The Church as the Body of Christ

The Church as the Body of Christ

BY EDUARD SCHWEIZER

 JOHN KNOX PRESS
RICHMOND, VIRGINIA

Scripture quotations, unless otherwise indicated, are from the Revised Standard Version, copyright 1946 and 1952 by the Division of Christian Education of the National Council of the Churches of Christ in the United States of America.

LIBRARY OF CONGRESS CATALOG CARD NUMBER: 64-16282

© M. E. BRATCHER 1964

PRINTED IN THE UNITED STATES OF AMERICA

9804(20)6399

CONTENTS

INTRODUCTION

Is it not irrelevant and untimely, in 1964, amid social
and political problems which have assumed massive
proportions and on which the existence of the world
itself might depend, to investigate the history of a Greek
word? Does this not signify an escape into the remote
past in order to avoid the urgent decisions of the present?

It is my hope that this book may manifest a little bit
of the relevance of such an investigation. To a great
extent the principal human decisions remain the same
throughout all centuries. Therefore, since the phenome-
non of language reveals some of these principal problems and answers of mankind, such an investigation may
help us to understand the manner in which other men
met the dangers and challenges of their lives. Thus we
may provide a valid criticism and correction for our own
ways of thinking and living.

I shall not investigate the problem of whether a specific understanding of man created some linguistic phenomena or whether, and in which way, some linguistic
facts led to a new understanding of man. My purpose
is a much more modest one. I try to describe what men,
particularly members of the early Christian church,
thought when they spoke about the body, and I try to
understand what basic ideas of man are involved in
such a thinking.

The following chapters form the body of four T. V.
Moore lectures delivered at San Francisco Theological

Seminary in April 1962. Detailed references to the passages quoted below are to be found in the author's article "Soma" in G. Kittel, *Theologisches Wörterbuch zum Neuen Testament,* Vol. VII.

Eduard Schweizer

I The Understanding of Man as Body— Greece and Israel

In Homer's writings the term "body" appears in Greek literature for the first time. Here it designates, probably exclusively, a corpse. This means that man experiences the body first as something alien to him, as a thing that is outside of himself, over which he stumbles. A corpse, of course, is never my own body, but the dead body of some other man or animal.

Since Hesiod, "body" also means the living body of man, often even the whole of his person. This concept of wholeness is to be found in the understanding of man as a "microcosmos," a "small world," and later in Stoicism, with which we shall deal presently. However, at this point a very characteristic usage emerges: since Demosthenes, "body" designates a slave, i.e., a thing which a man may own and dispose of. Thus a man may possess a hundred "bodies." A similar view is taken when one speaks of the god of war disposing of so many "bodies" or of a wrestler attacking four "bodies" at the same time. In a manner foreign to our feeling, the body is here primarily considered as a thing, as an object in front of us, and only secondarily as our own way of existing.

This becomes important, even in the time before Plato, when the body is clearly distinguished from the soul. The Orphic play on words, *soma-sema*, body-tomb, is taken over by Plato and is introduced by him into the Greek thought of subsequent centuries, thus influencing the thought of Europe and America to no small degree. This means that man, even when reflecting on his own body, is able to distinguish his essential ego from his body, so that the body still remains a kind of thing that one may see from a distance, without being personally identified with it.

This is certainly true for the earlier writings of Plato where the body is considered as a prison to which man is condemned, so that death only liberates him. The body is the evil principle which draws the divine soul down from heaven into the ruinous pleasures of sensuality.

In a later period of Plato's thought the beauty of the body may be considered as stimulating in a helpful way the spiritual ascension of the soul to the much higher ranks of the heavenly beauty of ideas. Yet the body remains an inferior thing, sometimes dangerous and seducing, sometimes stimulating and helpful, but nevertheless a part of man which must be left by his essential ego either in ecstasy or in death.

The further development of the usage of this word is determined by *Aristotle*. He is no longer able to believe in an independent existence of a soul separated from the body. Plato, in his *Timaeus*, could still try to combine metaphysics and science. Aristotle, although being definitely on the side of the latter, nonetheless remains a philosopher, dissatisfied by a mere description of nature. For him, a body, whether organic or inorganic, is determined by matter and form. Shapeless matter becomes body by its being formed into a specific object. The soul is the power that transforms matter into a living being, giving it its specific shape and existence. The physical body of man, without the soul, is nothing more than matter. The soul is a power confined to the body and non-existent outside of the body.

This leads to the *Stoic* concept of the body as that which is permeated by the soul. Since, for the successors of Aristotle, there is no immaterial soul, the soul must be conceived as bodily. Soul is body, a very fine, invisible body, but still body. In opposition to Aristotle, the Stoics are forced to state that two different bodies, namely the physical, fleshly body and the tender, almost immaterial, body of the soul, may be at the same place, permeating each other like fire and iron in a red-hot horseshoe. This life-giving, psychical body permeates not only the individual, but the whole world as well, in differing density, and may be called God. It appears in a stone as the power of coherence, in a plant as its nature, in an animal as its life, in man as his reason. Since this power is a creative body, one might speak of God the Creator, who is to be found everywhere in nature, but particularly and distinctively in the mind of man.

Furthermore, since this is a general power, there exists only one world-soul that appears in a specific body as its coherence, its nature, its life, or its reason, but never as an individual soul outside of a body. Not drawing all the consequences, the Stoics admitted that there might be a short period of an individual existence of man's soul after death, but this was little more than a compromise with popular expectations.

It is understandable that on this stage another usage

of the word "body" appears and becomes central from the third century B.C. up to the second century A.D. A close *relationship between the cosmos and man* is reflected in the earliest Greek language where the same word designates the roof of the world, the firmament, and the skull of man. Another word means "sky" and "palate"; another "wind" and "breath"; another the pillar supporting the sky and the uppermost vertebra of the human neck. Even before Plato, Democritus defined man as a microcosmos, a smaller world. Plato himself stated that the whole world is considered as a body, similar to the human organism. It is permeated and ruled by the divine reason which, like a world-soul, gives its life to the whole cosmos. The world is therefore an image of God, God rendered visible, the only-begotten one. This begets a new emphasis with the Stoics who see the whole cosmos as one single and harmonious unity held together and ruled by its divine world-soul. More and more the cosmos is understood as a giant body, the head of which, or the soul of which, is God. Hymns full of religious fervor praise this world which is identical with God. Zeus is, according to a fragment of Aeschylus, ether, earth, heaven, and all that exists beyond them. In the time of Paul, ether is the supreme God, head of the body, its ruler and mind. God contains the whole cosmos in himself and begets it out of himself. He has many names, but is the one God, destiny, and cosmos in one. Thus the world is a divine body, home and temple of God. As such it is a well-organized unity. The idea of a perfect form of wholeness, and a well-constructed organism, implied in the word "body," moves more and more into the foreground.

Since as early as the sixth century B.C., "body," in the

Greek language, has been used as a synonym for "shape" and even "idea." Plato used it to designate the well-structured *unity and wholeness* of a speech. After his time it connoted more and more any coherent unity, for instance a well-set tune, or a country united after having been dismembered by endless wars. The Stoic philosophers distinguished between (a) a body that is physically one, like an animal, (b) a body consisting of coherent things, like a ship or a house, and (c) a body consisting of separated unities, such as an army, a people, or an *ecclesia,* meaning in general "public meeting," but to a Christian "the church." However, prior to the fourth or fifth century A.D., the word "body" was never used as our English word is in such a connection as "a body of Romans," "a body of musicians," etc. A Greek in New Testament times could say that all soldiers together formed one body, or are one body, but he could not speak of a body of soldiers. T. W. Manson thought that he had detected one pre-Christian passage using "body" in this sense, but subsequent discussion has shown that the text has to be interpreted in a different way.

What is the result of this necessarily too scanty survey? In the time of the formation of the New Testament the dominant philosophy and its more popular layers led to an almost enthusiastic veneration of this world as a divine body and of man as a part of it. One cannot but be impressed by many of these witnesses to the deep religious feeling expressed in this concept of the divine world and the miracle of the divine mind of man.

And yet, this does not solve the problems of mankind.

If the world is a perfect organism, if man in his body is divine, there is no real "over against him." Such a philosophy would perhaps enable him to endure the evils of his time and the sufferings of his body. It would perhaps enable him to believe in his innermost kernel in spite of all that he has to suffer. It would perhaps be a most helpful philosophy as long as his sole aim would be merely his own peace.

But it would not enable him to get out of himself, to fight for something, to see his neighbor. And, in the long run, it would not be able to overcome his doubts about the perfect goodness of the world and of himself. It would leave him lonely in the face of the approaching death behind which nothing is to be expected. Is there really nothing else than my body which is permeated by a divine power and takes its place as a part of the greater world body?

Men who were not satisfied by this impressive view of the Stoics could, in the time of the New Testament, turn either to Epicurus or to Plato for an understanding of their body.

The Epicurean answer was simple. There is nothing but the body. There is no other goal of life than the bodily pleasures. To be sure, Epicurus' position was not as crude as his opponents stated. He was quite aware of the necessity of renouncing the extremely vehement desires in order to avoid evil results. He stressed the fact that the pleasures of the soul, which for him was only one part of the body, were higher than those of the flesh. This was not a moral evaluation, but one based on the fact that the pleasures of the soul secure a more poised and enduring pleasure. But though it be formulated in the noblest way, still the body was the only thing that mattered. Even if the pleasures offered by good music, famous poems, and works of art be the center of life, will this really offer assistance in enabling us to stand our life? There were few in the time of the New Testament who found an answer to their problems with Epicurus.

It is understandable that more and more people searched for this answer with Plato. We find a revival of Platonism in the time of Jesus and his apostles. With Plato there were to be found some higher values beyond this earth and this bodily existence. In the soul, man could find a part of the divine world, and yet not something that would end with the earthly body or simply endure as a general world-soul without any individuality. In his discussion of the origin of evil, Plato was able to explain how it came that evil was to be found in the body and in the world. Both body and world were the prison of the divine soul. At their best, the world and the body could assist the soul to escape, but more often they hindered such an escape by their power of seduction. There was a new meaning to life, namely that it was a worthwhile venture to fight for the purity of this soul against the bodily boundaries and allurements.

And yet, is this the answer? Is the body correctly understood when seen in opposition to the soul? Is its role a mere negative one? Is God more or less identical with man's soul and in opposition to his body? Is man here not torn into two separate parts? Has God nothing to do with one of these parts? Is the body a mere evil secluded from God and his acting? Is the earth only something from which one must escape?

One may ask the same questions with regard to *death*. Three principal answers were given in that time and are still prevailing among us.

First, the death of the body is simply considered as a natural event. The death of one man enables the life of others. Keep smiling, take it easy. It is as natural as sleep after a hard day's work. This would be the answer of Epicurus and his followers.

Second, the Greek language created the phrase "to die beautifully," which means that man considered the death of his body to be the last opportunity to stand the test and to show to himself and to the world how perfectly he was able to die. IIe proves his independence from all external attacks and dies as an hero transforming his death into the culminating point of his life. The concept of death of this kind could be found with many a Stoic philosopher.

Third, the death of the body is understood as the liberation of the divine soul to the real life in heaven with God, purified and blessed, far from the bodily sufferings and temptations. This, of course, was the Platonic answer. It is the naturalistic, the idealistic, or the specific religious (which does not mean Christian) answer to death, that is still to be found with men of today.

Are these the real answers? Or is there another answer in which we are not forced to choose among contenting ourselves with the pleasures of our body, or deifying it and its divine intellect, or contemplating it as evil and escaping into the realm of a bodiless soul? Let us turn to the Old Testament.

The Hebrew language possesses no word for "body." This may or may not have a direct relation to the undoubtedly different understanding of man in the Old Testament. It is at least notable that one of the most interesting of peoples did not create a specific word for "body," let alone a literature dealing with man in his bodily appearance or with the world as a divine body. To be sure, the Hebrew experienced his physical body as all men would do. But he did not reflect on it as, for instance, Greek men did. Is this simply a primitive stage of development or is this very fact a real and surprising answer to our problems? It may seem exaggerated to answer the latter question in the affirmative, and yet there is at least something of value in so doing. What does this fact mean?

After Aristotle, the Greek mind understood "body" by means of the terms "matter" and "form." Shapeless matter becomes a body when being formed into its specific shape. In the development of the Hebrew thinking, such distinction did not appear important. "Matter" and "form" are parts of a technical terminology. When defined by these terms, man is considered as a work of art in which one may watch the progress of shaping the intended form out of shapeless matter. This means that in thinking of man, the main interest focuses on himself, on his perfection or on the "more-or-less" of his approach to it. Man is compared with and measured both by the possibilities which lie in the substance out of which he is made, and by the vision of an ideal man that is the goal of his perfection. The Hebrew, when speaking of man, by implication means *man in the presence of God.* It is therefore not very important whether he is a bit closer to or a bit further away from a perfect specimen of man. He is always "flesh," mere creature, absolutely dependent on God's strength, limited, mortal, threatened by illness and death. "Flesh" in this sense is not a part of him, it is his very being, and never is he to forget that he is flesh for his whole life and in all his deeds and experiences. At the same time he always is "soul." Again, "soul" is not a part of him; he has no soul, he is soul. He exists because God created him as a living soul. God's sticking to him is his very life.

There is an impressive understanding of man to be found more than once in the Old Testament, where man is understood as living by the breath of God. God exhales, and man is inflated by life; God inhales, and man is dead (cf. Gen. 6:3; Ps. 104:29; Job 27:3; 34:14-15).

Only in the later parts of the Old Testament does the insight dawn that God sticks to man beyond death, not because there is some immortal part in himself, but because God keeps creating him as living flesh and as fleshly soul beyond the life in this aeon. Whether or not, when considered at face value, he is a more or less perfect body, seems not to be very important for the Hebrew. The only really relevant question is whether or not man, considered as created by and responsible to God, recognizes his status, his fleshliness as well as his soulness, and proves himself obedient to God.

Thus, neither the distinction between matter and form nor between body and soul is very important to the Hebrew mind. Man does not reach his goal in the perfection of his own personality, so that his life could be understood as the work of an artist who shapes the given matter into the most beautiful form. Nor is man allowed to retire into his innermost self in order to find there an immortal part of himself which would enable him to forget his fleshliness. In both understandings he would actually dispense with God. For he would find God in himself, in either his own creative power or in his immortal self.

The first possibility may lead to a deification of the body. Man remains lonely with his bodily ego, working on its perfection. Death, in this case, is either the natural end of this body, as with the Epicureans, or the last summit of perfection, so that dying itself becomes a perfect work of art, as with the Stoics.

The second possibility leads to a contempt of the body. Man finds his "self" apart from the body. Death in this case is liberation. All bodily life becomes unimportant, even a hindrance for the real life, as we found it with Platonism. Accordingly, licentiousness on the one hand and asceticism on the other are the two ideals proclaimed particularly in the late time of Hellenism around the turning of the aeons. Both understandings focus on the individual. The very word "body" may in Greek single out individuals, whereas in Hebrew the distinction between the one and the many is not of first importance, since man, in his dependence on and his responsibility to God, is at the same time seen in his dependence on and his responsibility to his fellowmen, his family, his tribe, his people.

When man considers himself as flesh and soul, regarding them not as two parts of his ego, but as two inseparable views of the same unity, he implies that considering man in and of himself, without God or his fellowmen as his "over-against-him," cannot possibly lead to a true understanding of himself. Man is man only when seen in the presence of God and his fellowmen. All contempt of the body is therefore impossible. It is created by God and brought to life by God's breath; it is a living soul. In it and nowhere else God wants to reveal his power, his grace, his faithfulness. It is the body of man that God will use to manifest his own glory. It is this very body in which man meets his fellowmen.

Yet, all deification of the body is equally impossible. Without God it is but flesh. Its frailty reminds man during his whole life of his absolute dependence on God. He cannot overcome death by his own power; he cannot flee to an innermost self, but only to God himself, on whom he is dependent even more in his death than in his life. And his fellowmen are not merely individuals which serve as yardsticks to measure the grade of his own perfection. They are the ones on whom he is always dependent, and to whom he is expected to render service.

And yet there was in the development of the Greek language an understanding of body that proved to be an excellent tool for expressing a new idea for which the Hebrew language had no equivalent term. We have seen that in the time of the New Testament, "body" frequently meant "unity," "wholeness," and that it was used particularly of the unity and wholeness of the cosmos.

At first sight, there seems to be an irreconcilable contrast. On the one hand, "body" in the Greek language serves to single out individuals, since "body" is the unity of one man, complete in himself, and needing no other relations. On the other hand, the fact that the Hebrew did not need any word for "body" shows that the distinction of his individual body from other human bodies was not of first importance for him. Man is flesh like all his fellowmen, even all the animals. He shares his mortality, his frailty, his creatureliness, with all men and animals. The Hebrew word *adam* means primarily mankind, and only secondarily individual man.

Thus, the Hebrew is used to seeing first the nation, the people, mankind, and only afterward the individual member of that nation, people, or mankind. It was Martin Buber who once observed that the Hebrew first sees the woods and only then single trees; whereas we in the Western world would see first the single tree, and only after a process of reflection do we call a thousand trees a wood. We Western people really miss the woods for the trees.

When children are tested to ascertain whether they are mature enough to enter school, they are asked for generalizing, comprehensive terms. In the Palestine of Old Testament times psychologists would probably have done the contrary and asked for terms of individuation. For the fact that the Hebrew language is poorer than the Greek in words singling out an individual is paralleled by the attitude of the Hebrew man who, naturally, without any special effort of mind, considers himself as a member of a whole people, not as an autonomous individual.

However, this very feeling of being incorporated into a much larger unity finds its linguistic expression in the Greek term "body" when used in a figurative sense for organic unity, not, as originally in Greek, of the individual body, but of a larger unity like a people or even the cosmos. When speaking of the unity of Christ's people, the New Testament will bring together both the Hebrew insight that man necessarily is incorporated into his people and into God's history with his people, and the Greek term "body" depicting such a unity in the image of a human body. In this way, the New Testament will speak of the body of Christ which is not an individual body, but a body including all its different members.

However, here a problem arises with which we shall later deal. For a Greek, "body" means necessarily the individual body of man and, in a figurative sense only, a larger unity which also conveys the image of a normal body of a human individual. For the Hebrew-speaking Jew, there is, strictly speaking, no concept of such an individual body at all. If he accepts and uses the Greek word "body" in this figurative sense, is it, for him, connected at all with a concept of an individual, physical body, or is it perhaps only a more or less abstract, general term, such as "unity," "wholeness"? In other words: Does he feel any connection with the earthly, individual body of Jesus, when he speaks of the body of Christ? Or does this phrase mean merely something like "Christian unity"?

II *The Body of Christ—Given for Many*

New Testament writers knew Old Testament background. In it, man is basically understood not as an individual, but in his relation to God and his fellowmen. This is, as we saw, combined with the fact that the Hebrew knew no specific word for "body." The Christians whose writings we possess in the New Testament spoke Greek. What usage did they make of this new tool that God gave into their hands?

Outside of Paul's letters, the word "body" appears relatively seldom. The only important development of the term is connected with its use in the words of the institution of the Eucharist. It is a well-known fact that there are two different types of tradition. According to Mark, only slightly altered by Matthew, both words run in a perfect parallelism: "This is my body—This is my blood of the covenant, which is poured out for many."

It is still a matter of dispute whether or not it is even possible to express the phrase "my blood of the covenant" in Aramaic. At least, it would be a rather clumsy phrase, and it is probable that the addition "of the covenant" was lacking in the underlying Aramaic phrase. According to Paul, again very slightly altered by Luke, the words run: "This is my body for you—This cup is the new covenant in my blood." The phrase "my body for you" is in Greek possibly even more awkward than in English, and probably impossible in Aramaic. It is likely to be a secondary addition made in the course of liturgical use in Greek-speaking congregations.

This reduces the problem to the alternative between a perfectly parallel form which equalizes bread and wine with body and blood, stressing the atoning effect of the blood shed for many, and a not so clearly paralleled form which connects the bread with the body and the cup with the new covenant in Jesus' blood. I am almost convinced that the latter form is the more original one.

It is perfectly understandable that a non-parallel form gets more and more paralleled in the course of a very intense liturgical use, whereas the contrary is not to be expected. This may be buttressed by the fact that all Swiss or American students whom I asked to quote these words out of their memory promptly quoted an even more paralleled form than we find anywhere in the New Testament, a mixture of Luke's first and Mark's or Matthew's second word.

One could, perhaps, explain the Pauline form as an alteration due to the abhorrence of a Jewish congregation of drinking blood. Yet exactly this speaks definitely against the originality of Mark's form identifying wine and blood. It is inconceivable that either Jesus or any Jewish congregation would have spoken of the wine as blood to be drunk, without, at the very least, pointing both to the special character of such an offense and to the reasons for overcoming such a stumbling block.

Besides, we know that with Jesus as well as with the early Jewish church the bread was distributed before the

23129

meal and the cup after it, so that both words were separated by the whole meal, as Paul's remark that Jesus took the cup "after supper" still emphasizes.

This explains why they were not quite parallel from the beginning. It also explains why in the first expression the body is mentioned, and in the second the covenant in Jesus' blood. For in both languages, in Greek and in Hebrew, there would be no linguistic basis for a close parallelism of "body" and "blood." It is exclusively the couple "flesh and blood" which is to be found, never the connection "body and blood." In the Pauline tradition which, by the way, is written a dozen years earlier than the Marcan report, "blood" appears in an additional remark only and is therefore not paralleled with "body."

Thus the oldest form of the words of institution probably stated that the bread was Jesus' body. If the Aramaic equivalent for "body," and not that for "flesh," was used, it meant that the bread was the token of his presence, since the Aramaic term includes both meanings, that of "body" as well as that of "self, ego." The second saying stated that Jesus' death was the token of God's willingness once again to enter into covenant with his people.

However, even earlier than the First Letter to the Corinthians, the common meal had been anticipated, and bread and wine had been distributed together at the end of the assembly because of practical needs. This means that the word about Jesus' body became closely associated with that about his blood. This necessarily led to an understanding in which the body was understood as the body of Jesus sacrificed for the sake of many, exactly as his blood was proclaimed in the second word

as poured out for many. Originally, the first word stressed
the presence of the Lord which gave to that meal its indescribable joy, the second word introduced the idea of
the new covenant with its eschatological connotations
and emphasized that Jesus' death on the cross was the
basis of that new life, so that the understanding of present, future, and past was implied, as it is today in all
four reports of the Lord's Supper in the New Testament.
The development which we described led to an understanding which focused more and more on Jesus' death.
We should remember that these words were repeated
week by week in the divine service, that they met the
ear of every Christian in what was perhaps the most distinguished moment of his week. Thus for the early Christian the idea of self-sacrifice for the sake of others was
definitely connected with the term "body," which is in
the history of this word a quite new and scarcely paralleled development. The bell that rang in the uncon-
scious of a Christian when he heard "body" rang something like "given for you" and not, as would be expected
in a Greek mind, anything like "perfect in itself, suitably
organized, well shaped."

When we turn to Paul, the first surprising result is
provided by statistical evidence. If we exclude the technical meanings of the word "body" used for "corpse" or
"slave," which, by the way, are not to be found with
Paul, there are 91 occurrences in Paul (including Ephesians and Colossians, excluding the Pastorals) over
against 51 in all other parts of the New Testament

(which, in the Greek New Testament, occupy four times more space than the Pauline letters). This shows how important the term is for Paul.

Yet the even more surprising fact is that within the undisputed letters, i.e., excluding Ephesians and Colossians which represent at any rate a later stage of Pauline thinking, nearly all occurrences of the word "body" are concentrated in the two Letters to the Corinthians and in the Letter to the Romans written in Corinth. "Body" occurs there 69 times, once in 1 Thessalonians, once in Galatians, and three times in Philippians. This shows that Paul's understanding of the body has been shaped in the discussion with his opponents in Corinth. This is one of the examples of the fact that even an extreme heresy was so often the pacemaker for a badly needed orthodox reinterpretation.

A year or two after Paul's first visit there, he discovered that they had reinterpreted his message in a highly Hellenized way. For the Corinthians the divine spirit was the only essential part of man. This led them to several consequences:

(a) No resurrection was needed, since man had become immortal and divine when he underwent baptism. Death meant merely that his deified self was freed from the physical body which had been his burden during earthly life (1 Cor. 15:12 ff.).

(b) The miracles happening in the congregation were the token of this deification. Particularly in the speaking in tongues, man escaped his bodily boundaries, his spirit moved in heavenly heights (1 Cor. 14).

(c) The body was an indifferent matter, even a nuisance. There were, on one hand, members of the church not daring to marry or to enter into marital intercourse (1 Cor. 7). There were, on the other hand, members to whom the body seemed so indifferent that they considered everything lawful, even prostitution and sexual immorality, as long as it did not touch the innermost divine self of man, his spirit (1 Cor. 6:12 ff.).

(d) *Gnosis,* knowledge, was the only thing that mattered, knowledge of this divine essence of man. Whether a fellowman got any help out of this or not was entirely unimportant. He interested the deified Christian only after having reached the same level of knowledge; otherwise he was a nuisance (1 Cor. 9:1 ff.).

(e) Like baptism, the Lord's Supper played a role of first importance, since it was considered as a medicine of immortality. The common meal, of course, was no consideration. It was utilized simply to appease the hunger, but had no significance for the life of the church. Why therefore wait for the latecomers (1 Cor. 11:17 ff.)?

Step by step Paul makes his way through such a misunderstanding of his preaching. There were real language problems that made an understanding difficult. Any Greek hearer of Paul's message would conceive of a life after death, if at all, as of a life of his soul or his spirit. "Body" for him would merely mean the conglomeration of bones and muscles that, of course, would discontinue living after death. On the contrary, Paul as a Greek-speaking Hebrew was scarcely able to think of any non-corporeal existence. "Body" meant for him real existence as over against a mere thought, an idea existing merely in the brain of somebody. This difference in perspective led Paul to clarify his position in the five points mentioned above:

(a) It caused a misunderstanding of the Corinthian idea of a psychical life going on after death. Paul obviously thought that they believed in nothing at all after death, which, of course, is impossible, since they underwent baptism for the sake of dead relatives or friends (1 Cor. 15:29). The answer of the Corinthians probably put this right. Nonetheless, Paul, in his second letter, has to insist on *the resurrection of the body*. It is certainly a different body, "a house not made with hands, eternal," yet it is body, it is not the abhorred nakedness which his opponents preached and which he, with his Old Testament background, could only detest and consider as an absolutely crazy idea. The much-debated passage, 2 Corinthians 5:3 ff., means nothing else than a restriction written between brackets: we long for that heavenly existence, provided that these crazy fellows in Corinth who assume a naked existence of the soul after death are not right. This means that Paul does not reflect about the question of whether his death would take place before the *parousia* or not, so that his expectation of a near parousia is probably the same as in 1 Corinthians 15:51 ff.

Why does Paul insist on the resurrection of the body? Is it only a Jewish leftover which we should abandon because we think much more in the manner of the Greek than of the Hebrew? Paul feels that there is something entirely wrong in treating the body with such a contempt and in so overvaluing the soul.

First, it means that our eternal life lies in ourselves. Man ceases to credit God with the gift of the eternal life when he begins to speak of his own immortal soul.

Second, it is not sober thinking. "Soul" means either something like our psyche or something which is absolutely unimaginable and indescribable. In the first case death would mean that man was freed from his corporeal part, whereas his psychical part with all its complexes (inferiority complexes, father complexes, mother complexes, etc.) lived on. It would be hard to tell whether this would not be worse than having our body with its toothaches into all eternity. In the second case "soul" remains an absolute blank, and Paul's interpretation, which sees the continuity between the old earthly and the new risen man in God's faithfulness that will re-create man after the death of body and soul, seems clearer and easier to understand.

Third, a fellowship of mere souls would not mean much to Paul. Real community necessarily includes some bodily manifestation, for instance a common meal. A fellowship of souls without any bodily means of expression, without words, acts, signs, is no fellowship at all. Therefore, being together with Christ will come to its fullness only when our bodies have become like his glorious body and share in a very concrete way his heavenly existence (Phil. 3:21).

Fourth, this concept implies the danger of neglecting the body and its acts during this earthly life. Just in that passage, 2 Corinthians 5:1-10, Paul emphasizes that the new life is not simply a natural prolongation of our deified self. Only through judgment we shall reach it. And before the throne of the heavenly Judge it is exactly the deeds that we did "in the body," on the basis of which we shall be judged (5:10). In the body lies every opportunity of serving God or of rejecting him.

Just because the body will be raised by God, it is so utterly important whether we use it in God's service or not (Rom. 6:12; 8:11; 1 Cor. 6:14). To express it in modern terms: It is absolutely unimportant whether we imagine that spiritual body as more or less material or as immaterial. But *it is extremely important to know that we shall live exclusively by God's own act of creation* which gives us our new body and our new soul, i.e., our whole eternal life, not simply a new house for our own soul that does not have to go through any death. It is equally important to know that our self is a bodily self, i.e., that *the whole of our earthly life, including our corporeal acts no less than our thinking and feeling, really matters*, because we ourselves will be before God's throne, not simply some part of us. Both our physical and our corporeal deeds or experiences will be present in the last judgment. Both will go through that judgment, so that we, bodily and psychically, shall live only by God's gracious new creation act.

(b) One of the most pregnant decisions made by Paul is his reinterpretation of the term "spirit" in 2 Corinthians 12:1 ff. He begins with the statement that supernatural phenomena like speaking in tongues or other ecstatic experiences occurred also in the former lives of the people in heathen cults. These phenomena may or may not be used by God. The otherworldliness, in the sense of the Corinthians, of such experiences depends much on the temperament and the heritage of the people involved, even on the climate in which they are living, and is certainly no guaranty of their divine origin. The yardstick to be used when testing these gifts is not whether they are more or less natural or supernatural, known or unknown, but whether they proclaim Jesus as Lord, or in other words: whether they build up the church (1 Cor.

12:2 ff.; 14:4). Therefore the "normal" gifts meeting the bodily needs of men are as high as those which are exercised in a more spiritual reach. The service rendered to those in need appears second in listing in Romans 12:7, directly after the gift of prophecy and before the gift of teaching. The list in 1 Corinthians 12:28 includes administrators and helpers, although verses 12:29 ff. show that these gifts are not aimed at by the Corinthians.

(c) The Corinthians imagined that religion had to do with the non-corporeal reaches of man only. In some way man was considered here like a department store with different levels, where one finds pants and stockings on the ground floor, hymnbooks and other spiritual things on the fifth. In opposition to such a view, Paul stresses the fact that it is his physical body in which he carries the death of Jesus, and in which the life of Jesus will be manifested (2 Cor. 4:10). He explains this by pointing to the sufferings to which he is subject. He really bears the marks of Jesus, namely the scourging scars on his body (Gal. 6:17). This reversely creates life. For on one hand the pre-eminent glory of God is to be seen only in the earthly vessel of Paul's body (2 Cor. 4:7). The contrast of this suffering body, living day by day in danger of death, reminds the congregation that the rock of their faith is the Lord, not a frail man. On the other hand these experiences, still visible on his body, credit his message. They show the genuineness of the faith preached by Paul.

The death of Jesus suffered in Paul's body becomes the life of Jesus in the faith of the congregation (2 Cor. 4:11 ff.). Or in the words of 2 Corinthians 1:3-11—which is one of the outstanding texts dealing with the problem of suffering—first, only a man knowing bodily pains and needing consolation is able to console in his turn. Second, the suffering of the apostle leads to a communion of prayers. Third, facing death corroborates faith in God who raises the dead.

It is so important that man lives his faith in his body, even pommels and subdues it lest, in preaching to others, he himself would be disqualified (1 Cor. 9:27).

It is a most illuminating fact that the term "body" appears very often when Paul turns from the indicative mood to the imperative. Thus, in Romans 12:1, after having emphasized how much God's mercies mean to us, Paul goes on: "I appeal to you . . . by the mercies of God, to present your bodies as a living sacrifice . . ." The bodies are the place in which the cult of the church, its "spiritual worship" takes place, and it is illuminating again that cultic language appears with Paul almost exclusively in the context of the everyday life of the church and never describing what we should call a church service. In Romans 6:12 ff. also the word "body" turns up as the apostle repeats the statements about Christ's death and life, but now, these statements are in the imperative mood, showing that his death and life go on in our bodies, since believing in it means living by it in our bodily existence. Again, the term "body" does not mean a special part of man, but the whole of him in his earthly and therefore bodily life. This is shown by the fact that the expression "your bodies" in 6:12 alternates with the pronoun "yourselves" in 6:13. It is in man's physical body that Christ will be glorified whether by martyrdom or by a life of service (Phil. 1:20).

The most interesting and surprising passage is 1 Corinthians 6:12-20. Man's body is the temple of God's Spirit, the means for glorifying God. It is not the soul, it is the body, including the soul, which is bought by Christ. Therefore it belongs to him as he belongs to the body.

Most unexpected, however, is Paul's statement that sexual immorality is the most weighty sin because it involves the body as no other sin does. This is only understandable if one realizes two facts: First, it is exactly in this context that Paul distinguishes carefully the body from the belly. Digestion usually goes on without touching my ego at all. Sexuality, on the contrary, always involves my body, i.e., the whole of my existence. It never is something which simply happens, from which I could sever my innermost self. The stomach, of course, is part of my person, but I may consider it as in some way separated from myself. It usually does its work while I am involved in works or thoughts which are in no way related to it. The same would not be true for my sexual life, or the very fact that my innermost self were not involved would by itself be a sign of perversion. Thus, the term "body" in this context means the whole personality, not merely bones, muscles, and glands. And it follows that sexuality, for Paul, is by no means a mere glandular function.

Second, Paul distinguishes the body from the spirit or mind of man. It means the whole person as it lives here on earth in contact with all fellowmen. My thoughts or my feelings may or may not touch the lives of my fellowmen; they may happen in a realm far away from my everyday life and the lives of my neighbors. My sexuality always involves my partner. It may even include an absent or a still future spouse. Because, for Paul, faith always has to be lived in our concrete existence, particularly in the togetherness with other men, sexuality is for him a means of first importance for expressing one's faith.

From this point of view, 1 Corinthians 6:15 becomes clear: "Do you not know that your bodies are members of Christ? Shall I therefore take the members of Christ and make them members of a prostitute?" This membership of Christ is certainly not a mystical experience, a reality to be expressed in mysterious language conceivable by adepts only. What Paul wants to say is very simple indeed. He underlines merely the fact that the connection between Christ and his disciples is so intimate that it involves one totally, or in Paul's terms: bodily. Therefore it is simply impossible that this body bought by Christ, and thus being his property, should be thrown away to a prostitute. His opponents in Corinth considered sexuality an indifferent matter, since it did not touch man's spiritual life. Paul, on the contrary, sees in it one of the most significant expressions of our life, since it necessarily involves other men, either damaging their lives or giving them new strength and joy.

(d) For the Corinthians, spiritual knowledge was the only goal. Men were of interest exclusively as teachers of this knowledge. They became unimportant, even hindrances, as soon as one had got the knowledge that they were able to communicate. After what we have said in the preceding paragraph, we may be brief. 1 Corinthians 8 shows that any knowledge belonging to a spiritual reach only and forgetting the demands of this earthly life, for instance the needs of our fellow Christians, is only puffing up, not building up (8:1). If a man, out of his spiritual insight, acts in a way that hurts or even destroys other members of the congregation, he sins directly against Christ who died for these other members (8:11-13). The same is said in an even more urging way in the famous chapter 13, the song of love.

(e) Finally, the Eucharist, for the Corinthians, was something like a sacramental meal of a mystery religion, imparting immortality. Fellowship therefore was totally unimportant, the sacrament being an individual feeding with divine food nourishing the immortal soul. In opposition to that, Paul insists on the fact that they actually destroyed the sacrament by having destroyed the fellowship meal. There is certainly no question of the Corinthians not being reverent enough toward the sacrament. All that we read in Paul's first letter to them points to the contrary. They even baptized themselves for the dead (15:29), and they had to be reminded that sacraments did not guarantee salvation magically (10:1 ff.). The whole passage 11:17-34 contains but one reproach: that they celebrated the Lord's Supper without waiting for the latecomers (11:21 at the beginning, and 11:33 at the end). These latecomers were those who had nothing (11:22), the slaves who were not allowed to leave early enough to arrive in time for the meeting of the church. Paul is sober enough to understand that it is hard to be seated at a full table hungry and to wait for these poor brothers. He therefore admonishes them to eat and drink at home before going to the meeting. For anyone who eats the bread or drinks the cup in an unworthy manner, namely, forgetting his poor and humiliated brothers and their most real earthly hunger, will be guilty against the body and blood of the Lord given for these very brothers (11:27).

There is in the Greek text no basis at all for inserting the idea of a profanation of the body and blood. The reasoning is exactly the same as in chapter 8 with which we just dealt. Thus, body and blood stand for "Christ who died for the brother." Celebrating the Eucharist without caring for the poor brothers, at least so much that one waits for them to get a real meal like all others, is sin against the Lord himself who sacrificed his body and blood for the least of his brethren.

A practice which separates the sacrament from the brotherhood meal turns the former into a strange, almost heathen rite which totally lacks its "bodily" expression in the context of the whole life of its participants, and it turns the latter into a mere social affair which lacks any real depth and could be found equally well in a bowling club. A Lord's Supper without a church supper is perhaps not quite, but almost, as bad as a church supper without a Lord's Supper!

We may conclude. There are, before the New Testament, a few passages speaking about giving up one's body for God's sake. But they are mostly to be found in Hellenistic writings differentiating soul and body in such a way that the body is considered as the burden that has to be sacrificed willingly in order to liberate the divine soul. The stress does not lie on the help given to others or the praise rendered to God, but rather on the unworthiness of the body. In the New Testament, the use of the term "body" in the liturgy of the Lord's Supper had a creative effect on the understanding of the role of our body. As the word has rarely been used before in connection with sacrifice or self-sacrifice, it probably did not imply at first a sacrificial nuance, although it described, from the very beginning, the presence of that Lord who sacrificed himself, according to the Jewish scheme, on the same day on which he celebrated the last meal with his disciples. Originally, the word "body" simply denoted the self of Jesus Christ, his person, being present at any future table of Eucharist, giving to each future meal its character of eschatological joy and exultation. In the course of the development that combined the eating of bread and drinking of wine at the end of the meal, the words "body" and "blood" became parallel. The term "body" still designated the whole person of Jesus Christ, as long as the Old Testament background was not totally abandoned. However, it meant more and more the person of Jesus Christ as it was sacrificed for the sake of many, the person of Jesus Christ in its importance for those for whose sake he had died and had been raised.

Thus the first step in a new understanding of the body was the fact that the early Christians learned from their Master that his body was the means by which he, in his whole personality, lived and died for the sake of others. This was an understanding appropriate to their Old Testament background, where man is essentially seen as a unity in his relation to God and his fellowmen. Therefore neither the idea that the body is only a part of man to be distinguished from his soul, nor the idea of the body as a world perfect in and of itself, presented itself to the New Testament Christians.

The second important step was taken by Paul who

met in Corinth an interpretation of Christianity in terms of individual salvation that neglected all relations to other men. Fighting such a misunderstanding, the apostle stressed the importance of man's body as the place on which, and the means by which, he lives his faith toward his fellowmen. Urged by this misrepresentation of his message, he took up the idea of the body of Jesus given to serve many, and understood the human body as that side of our total existence by which we contact others, meet them, serve them, build up a congregation, or enter into fellowship with the world.

Looking back to the different shades of meaning which the word "body" took in Greek and to the fact that a Hebrew word for "body" was lacking so that the understanding of the body had to be expressed in other terms, we may say that much of the Old Testament understanding of man is still predominant. Man is seen as a totality. His bodily existence within the human society is considered more important than his individual inner life in which he is alone with himself. Or to be precise: This latter is important as far as it leads him to get back into the world of his fellowmen better prepared for serving them. Neither the Epicurean or Stoic deification nor the Platonic contempt of the body could be the basis of the New Testament view of man. However, the Hebrew view also underwent some change. Although man in the Old Testament had always been understood as being in the presence of God, living to serve him and his fellowmen, the term "body" was missing, and the more or less equivalent term "flesh" underlined only the creatureliness of man, his boundaries, his frailty, his exposure to illness and death. The Greek differentiation between "flesh" and "body" enabled the apostle to see in the body that side of man's existence which certainly has its weakness and reminds him of his total dependence on God, but is first of all the means to glorify God in serving men, the place on which faith is lived in a concrete way building up the church of God. Just because Paul cannot think of any existence which would not be bodily existence, he understands that man as body is man in his openness to God and his neighbors. Therefore the body, in spite of all its limits and frailties, is the place in which God will be glorified.

III *The Church as the Body of Christ*

It makes little difference for our inquiry whether we consider the Letters to the Colossians and Ephesians as written by Paul, or by one of his intimate disciples, so that the Corpus Paulinum would be more of a teamwork than we usually suppose. At any rate they show a later stage of the development of Pauline thought. Therefore it is methodically sound to concentrate in this chapter on Paul's undisputed letters and to deal with Colossians and Ephesians in the following.

The astonishing result of even a superficial investigation is that in the undisputed letters there is, besides the liturgical phrases of the Eucharist, but one passage in which Paul properly speaks of "the body of the Christ," using both articles. This passage is Romans 7:4: "You have died to the law through the body of the Christ" (author's translation). Besides that there is only the phrase in 1 Corinthians 12:27 which literally reads: "You are body of Christ." However, the omission of the articles may be due to its status as predicate, although the articles are not impossible if the uniqueness of the predicate should be stressed. Be this as it will, it is at any rate only one more occurrence to which we shall turn later.

41

Let us begin with Romans 7:4. One should not doubt that Paul was thinking of Jesus' body that died on the cross in order to free us from the law. For in chapter 7 he deals at some length with what it means to live under the law, and at the beginning of chapter 8 he explains how God overcame the curse of the law in the flesh of Jesus executed on the cross.

The same meaning is to be found in the Eucharist texts. The typical Pauline form of the words of institution is illuminating. In a rather clumsy way he, or perhaps the church even before him, adds to the word "body" the phrase "for you," so that the saying is: "This is my body for you." This linguistically awkward form is chosen in order to express the meaning of the word unmistakably: the body of Christ is his body which has been killed on the cross for our sake. It is hence not considered as an object which would be interesting in itself, but rather as the source of a stream going out of it. One would therefore be wrong investigating merely the historical fact telling us something about a past event in Palestine. For this undoubtedly historical fact has its value in its meaning for us, for the church of today.

We have seen how the understanding of the body underwent a rich development in the early church. It was particularly the liturgy of the Eucharist which, Sunday by Sunday, told the church that the body of Jesus had been given for the sake of the church.

More and more, the body has been understood as the means of rendering service to one's fellowmen. In connection with Jesus, the word "body" even meant, for these Christians, almost his act of sacrifice for the sake of the many. In this sense and with this effect the body of Christ nailed to the cross in Palestine, whether twenty or two thousand years ago, is still present. This is not to be understood as a magical or mystical or in any other way mysterious representation in itself. Whether the importance of that death for us is thought of in terms of sacrificial atonement, of definite revelation of God's love toward mankind, or even of pioneer work enabling us to follow on the path of love, it means that this body is present in its importance for us. This is to be found in both the stream of God's love, established there once and for all, and continuing like a source springing from there, and in the challenge to the obedience of faith, founded in the lordship of Christ to which he was raised and which he is still exercising. Both blessing and challenge still emanate from the death and resurrection of Jesus Christ and meet the congregation assembled in the celebration of the Lord's Supper. In the words "This is my body for you" the intended effect of that death on the cross is expressed and so transmitted to the church. Listening to this declaration, the church receives with the bread the blessing and the challenge which this crucified and risen body of Christ procures.

This is probably more evident for the mind of an early Christian than for ours. Time for him was not a theoretical line divided by hours which follow each other as regularly as our watches run, so that an hour is always of exactly the same length. He, of course, never looked at his wristwatch, thinking: "It is now 5:10; it takes ten minutes to the station so that I should get the 5:20. As it is a ten-minute ride, I shall arrive at 5:30. Allowing ten minutes for walking home, I am pretty sure to arrive at 5:40." Nor would he use this method for counting the years; this was even more true for a Palestinian than for a Hellenist or a Roman. An average Palestinian would not employ a reasoning like ours: "This event took place in 1954—that one was two years earlier, so it must have been 1952." He said: "This happened in the year of the earthquake," and his wife replied: "Oh, no, it was the year of the famine."

Years have everywhere different characters and qualities just as men do; but in a culture in which one does not count the years or counts them only within short periods, e.g., within the reign of one king, this character of years moves much more into the foreground of one's thinking.

A second observation goes deeper. Is it not true that a past event is often much more present than some contemporary events? The fact that my mother prayed with me forty years ago is still present in my life, whereas the fact that a bus is speeding through New York's Fifth Avenue at this very minute is not present for me in any meaningful way.

The same is true in regard to future events. Sitting in the waiting room of a dentist's office is different from sitting in a cafeteria. This is so, not because the present circumstances are different—the easy chair may be even more comfortable and the magazines even more interesting at the dentist's than in the cafeteria. The future events, the dentist's drilling or the sweetness of the expected pastries, are somehow present before they actually happen.

Again this is probably even more in the foreground of a Hebrew mind and easier to understand for him, since his verb has no real tenses distinguishing "I eat" from "I ate" or "I shall eat." Of course, one may circumscribe a past or a future time by some addition, and usually the context makes clear what time is meant. And yet, he would be accustomed to all the prophetic texts in his Bible in which the coming action of God is described as if it had already happened. The structure of his language and the biblical idea that a future action of God is absolutely certain as soon as God has decided to act probably co-operated in shaping his understanding of time. In a similar way the deliverance from Egypt through the Red Sea is a still present fact, since Israel is still living because of this redeeming act of God. Past, present, and future are not necessarily and distinctly separated from each other.

If we apply this to the body of Jesus, nailed on the cross, it is clear that this is, for an early Christian, never simply that physical body of bones and muscles which had been buried many years ago. It was that very body, sacrificed for him and thereby present as the basis of his whole life, both blessing him and challenging him. It is present in its blessing still going on: "The cup of blessing which we bless, is it not a participation in the blood of Christ? The bread which we break, is it not a participation in the body of Christ?" (1 Cor. 10:16). And it is present in the challenge still going on: "Whoever eats the bread and drinks the cup in an unworthy manner (namely in contempt toward his fellow members) will be guilty against the body and blood of the Lord (which had been given some twenty years ago for the sake of these fellow members today)" (1 Cor. 11:27, author's translation). In all these passages the body of Christ is certainly the body of Jesus nailed to the cross. However, this is not to be severed from the risen body, since the crucified body of Jesus is only important in its blessing and challenging effect which meets us in the blessing and challenge of the risen Christ. That the risen Lord as the one to whom one may even pray is certainly more than the mere effect of his death on the cross, is clear, but is not to be discussed here.

Thus we may say that for Paul the crucified body of Jesus Christ includes all that is the result of this act. It is *the crucified body in its for-our-sake-ness*. The truth of this is based on the fact that God raised Jesus from the dead. Or to express it in another image: the crucified body of Jesus is the place in which man finds sense to his life, because the crucified Jesus becomes for him the token of God's incredible love and the challenge to service which makes his life meaningful. Again, the truth of this is manifested in the resurrection in which Jesus proved to be not dead, but a living Lord of the church.

Thus, we may understand how this body of Christ is, for Paul, something like a sphere, a realm, a reach, into which man has to go or to be put in order to find his life. Or to say it again in another term: it is the church, understood as the place, the realm, the sphere, in which Jesus, crucified but raised two thousand years ago, is still telling us of God's love, and is still challenging us and calling us under his lordship.

Thus the term "body of Christ," in its essential meaning, comes close to the word "church." However, all this does not yet explain why Paul, in 1 Corinthians 12:27, is able to state: "you are the body of Christ." One could easily say, for instance, that the blood of Christ is still present in the church, that somehow it means the bless-

ing and challenge by which the church lives, that the
church therefore is saved and is living "in the blood of
Christ"; but one could not formulate: "you are the blood
of Christ" as one may formulate: "you are the body of
Christ."

Let us start with Romans 12:5. The context there is
much the same as in 1 Corinthians 12. Paul admonishes
the congregation to be one and to use the manifold gifts
of the Spirit for the building of this unity. As in 1 Corinthians 12:27, he grounds this summons in the fact that
"we, though many, are one body in Christ." Any Greek
could have said: "we, though many, are one body." This
would not mean more than: "we form a coherent unity."

The Stoics used the very word *ecclesia*, "public meeting," as an example of a united body being composed of
different independent persons. The same word *ecclesia*
designates the church in early Christianity. Hence the
first part of Romans 12:5 does not express anything new
and would be evident for any Greek reader contemporary with Paul. But a Gentile, of course, would never
have added the last two words.

For Paul, on the contrary, these two words are the
decisive ones: "we are one body *in Christ.*" What do
they mean?

Let us start from quite a different angle. In pre-
Christian Judaism, for instance in Psalm 80, Israel had
been described as *the vine of God.* In the contemporary
Jewish book telling the Bible stories in a popular form,
namely in Pseudo-Philo's *Biblical Antiquities,* Israel ap-

pears as the cosmic vine of God whose roots reach down into hell and whose branches reach up into heaven. The people of God is something like the giant body of a vine permeating the whole cosmos from hell to heaven. Or to say the same without image: the life and destiny of the whole cosmos, of men, demons, and angels, depend upon and are tangent to the people of God, Israel.

In the New Testament a similar image appears. John 15:1 ff. speaks of *the true vine*, i.e., the unique, the only one, in which life and salvation are to be found. But who is this vine? Shall we say: the church, the new Israel? This would not be wrong, but neither would it be precise. For the chapter begins with Jesus' saying: "I am the true vine . . . I am the vine, you are the branches. . . . apart from me you can do nothing." This is nothing else than the insight that the church, because of Jesus Christ, is all that it may be. It is actually living "in him," exclusively "in him." As the branches are fruit-bearing branches only because they are "in" the vine, engrafted into its stem, the church lives in its Lord, "in Christ."

We may even go a few steps further into the background of John. Little more than a scribal error has probably suggested this identification of Jesus and the vine of God. For, as C. H. Dodd points out, in Psalm 80:16 the Son of man and the vine of God, Israel, are identified by a slip of a very early copyist, whose traces are to be found in all extant Hebrew and Greek texts of that Psalm. This is important because it shows that the idea of the Christ-vine embracing the whole church is rooted in a Son of man Christology which still can be traced in the background of some parts of the Fourth Gospel. Another text of this same layer is John 1:51: ". . . you will see heaven opened, and the angels of God ascending and descending upon the Son of man." This is certainly a reinterpretation of Genesis 28:12. Not only do angels appear nowhere else in John's Gospel (5:4 is to be omitted), except once in the tradition of the resurrection; not only is the strange sequence "ascending and descending" the same as in Genesis 28; but even more important is the fact that the Rabbis explained the text in Genesis 28:12 in a way which makes it a close parallel to John 1:51. They understood the phrase "the angels of God were ascending and descending on it [the ladder]" in the sense that they ascended and descended upon him (Jacob). As the Hebrew *bo* can mean "on him" as well as "on it," this interpretation is equally possible grammatically. This would mean that in John 1:51 the Son of man takes exactly the place of the forefather Jacob, so that this text is in some way related to the tradition in chapter 4, which contrasts Jesus with the patriarch Jacob. Jacob, of course, is only one of the names of this ancestor. The other and more important one is Israel. Jesus hence is, as the Son of man, the new Jacob or the new Israel, the new patriarch who bears in himself the new people of God.

This is certainly no far-fetched idea. In the Book of Jubilees, Jacob plays an eminent role. His name is elected as that of the firstborn of God as early as the creation (2:20). Jacob is forefather and tribe at the same time: "The Lord will elect him [namely, "my son Jacob"] for his own people," and he will be "his firstborn son and his people for ever" (19:28 ff.). The blessings of God are even said to remain on the parting of the hair of Jacob's tribe (22:13), which is a very strange image. It shows to what extent the tribe is understood as an individual man represented in its ancestor. This Jacob is, according to Jubilees, the head of mankind like Adam, Enoch, Noah, and Sem (2:13, 23; 19:24, 27), and through him the whole cosmos, heaven and earth, will be renewed (19:25). In 2 (4) Ezra, written towards the end of the first century A.D., Jacob is the symbol of the new aeon, and with Philo, the older contemporary of Jesus, he is even the first creature of the unoriginated beings, which seems to be a contradictio in adjecto, but so it is (De Posteritate Caini 63); he is furthermore the symbol of those who arrive at seeing God directly (De Praemiis et Poenis 43-46). He, Jacob, by his divine name, Israel, is a heavenly being, higher than all angels; he is both the Logos and the heavenly Adam (De Confusione Linguarum 146). In all these texts we are rather close to the idea that the patriarch Jacob, blessed by God, contains in himself a whole people or even a mankind blessed by God, and that he is at the same time a heavenly being. When the first Christians considered themselves as the new, eschatological Israel, and knew that they were such exclusively because of the Son of man Jesus Christ, the figure of the new Jacob-Israel, embracing in himself a new people, presented itself at once.

When these Christians understood that this new people of God was not only a new Israel, but rather a new mankind, it would be the figure of a new Adam rather than that of a new Jacob offering itself for such a concept. As early as Philo, the heavenly Adam and the heavenly Israel-Jacob have been identified, as we have seen. In the Qumran writings the original glory of Adam that had been lost since the fall is believed to be reestablished in the eschatological community of Qumran, subsequent to the judgment and the purification from all sins. It will consist of "knowledge of the Highest" and "wisdom of the sons of heaven" (IQS 4.21-23; IQH 17.15; IQpPs 37.11.2; Damasc. 3.20[5.6]). In early Christianity it was again a group that saw in Jesus the Son of man, which identified him with the new, the eschatological, Adam initiating a new mankind. This, of course, was only the more universalistic version of the same concept which considered the Son of man the new Jacob-Israel. This group is to be found in the background of Paul.

For in both passages where Paul deals with the idea of Christ being the eschatological Adam the idea of Christ being the one man or the Son of man is also still visible. Nowhere else does it occur, since the Son of man title is inconceivable for Greek-speaking people, and consequently Paul never uses it. But in Romans 5:15, Jesus, in contrast to Adam, is called "that one man." First Corinthians 15:27, mindful of the same contrast, Psalm 8, which speaks of the "son of man," is, without any further explication, related to Jesus Christ, presupposing, without mentioning the term itself, that he is the "son of man" of Psalm 8. This proves that a group of early Christians, living before Paul and John composed their writings, confessed Jesus as being the Son of man and inaugurating a new Israel or a new mankind. In the former case he would be called the eschatological Jacob, in the latter, more universalistic view, he would be the eschatological Adam.

Let us, after this long detour, go back to the phrase in Romans 12:5 which states that we, though many, are one body in Christ. The first Christians expressed in various images their conviction to be the new Israel or the new mankind of God, in him, in Jesus Christ. Even this expression "in him" is not unheard of. "In him," namely either the good or evil spirit, are the generations of mankind, according to the Qumran writings (IQS 4.15). The church is in the True One; "in the evil one" is the world, according to 1 John 5:19. And Hebrews 7:4-10 states that all Levites had been in the loins of Abraham when he met Melchizedek. According to the Rabbis, Israel is elected in Abraham, and the whole world has been collected in Adam by God when he created him.

This is due to the well-known fact that, in the time of the New Testament, the more Hellenistic concept of space is superseding more and more the original Hebrew concept of time. Thus Paul in Galatians 4:25 ff. contrasts the present Jerusalem not with the coming, but with the heavenly, one, speaking in the first part of his thread of thought in temporal categories, in the second in spatial ones. Therefore the phrase "in Christ," though being, strictly speaking, a local expression defining the spot, the reach, the sphere, in which something exists, actually points to the Christ whose history determines all those who live "in him."

The best proof for this is the surprising observation that the closing phrase in chapters 5 to 8 in Romans alternates twice between "in Christ" and "through Christ." Both expressions mean exactly the same. A congregation is "in Christ" if it is in the reach of the blessing and challenge still emanating from the history of Jesus Christ, from his crucifixion and his resurrection, so that it lives

"through Christ," through his redeeming acts, his cruci-
fixation, and his resurrection.

This explains why for Paul *the body of Christ* means
*the real body of flesh nailed on the cross as well as the
church.* In 1 Corinthians 10:16 ff. he is hence able to
move from one meaning to the other without any break
or even a hint of a change in the understanding: "The
bread which we break, is it not a participation in the
body of Christ? Because there is one bread, we who are
many are one body, for we all partake of the one bread."

The first sentence is probably a liturgical text taken
up by Paul, whereas the second one gives his own interpretation. The crucified and risen body of Jesus is the
basis of the church, almost the event which created and
is creating it. It is, for a mind trained in Old Testament
thinking, Jesus himself in his for-our-sake-ness, or Jesus
including all of his believers. The idea of the patriarch
containing in himself the whole tribe, because he determines its destiny, helped to form the expression of the
"body of Christ." This is particularly true for the concept of both Jacob-Israel being at the same time an individual forefather and the whole of the people, and
Adam, understood as an individual man at the beginning
of the world and equally as whole mankind. Both had
in the time of Paul and John been identified with each
other and with a heavenly being called Logos or Word
of God. This Logos who is the heavenly Adam and the
heavenly Jacob-Israel, is more or less the same as the
figure which is more often named Sophia, the heavenly
Wisdom, pre-existant since the creation of the world,
descending to earth, calling men to repent, rejected by
them, and returning to heaven. These Jewish speculations make it easily understandable that the first Chris-

tians understood Jesus Christ as the new patriarch embracing a new people or a new mankind.

But what does all this mean? It seems to me to be important in its theological implications, for it shows that the idea of the church as the body of Christ has nothing to do with the idea of an extension of Christ himself in his church. We shall later deal with some conclusions to which the body of Christ conception led in Colossians and Ephesians. But for the moment we must emphasize that Paul did not combine any concept of a mystical unity with the idea of the church being the body of Christ. Such a conception was supposed when scholars explained it as originating from a Gnostic myth about a giant body of the Redeemer in which all saved souls are substantially included, being united by their same divine nature in a way not visible for unilluminated eyes. This Gnostic myth has probably never existed. At least the term "body" in this sense is lacking even in later Gnostic books, except in Christian writings, undoubtedly influenced by Paul. There is but one occurrence of the word "body" in a typically Gnostic context, in which this could perhaps be interpreted in the mentioned sense, and even this is a collection of sayings of Christian Gnosticism, namely *Excerpta e Theodoto* 42. Even if we do not look for the very term "body," but rather for the idea of such a body of souls in a broader sense, there are only a very few traces of the concept of souls forming a compact unity with the Redeemer. The prevailing idea seems to be that they are merely of the same substance as this one. Thus, the conception of a mythological, physical unity of Redeemer and redeemed seems not to be at the root of the Pauline body of Christ.

This means that the church is the body of Christ, because it lives by all that has been done by Jesus Christ for its sake. It is united with him by the fact that his history, namely his life and death and resurrection, is the foundation of the church's life, without which it would not exist at all. The church exists in the body of Christ or through the body of Christ crucified and risen for the sake of the world, still present in its blessing and challenge, for instance when the Eucharist is celebrated. Outside of this body of Christ, given for its sake, the church does not exist. The saying in 1 Corinthians 12:27: "You are the body of Christ," and the surprising end of verse 12 in the same chapter: ". . . just as the body is one and has many members . . . so it is with Christ," are possible because the idea that a whole tribe is included in its ancestor is familiar to Paul. Hence these sayings describe the total dependance of the church on its founder, on Jesus Christ, in a most impressive way.

The term recommends itself particularly when the unity of the congregation is stressed, since the term "body" designates in Greek the wholeness, unity, and totality of a conglomeration. As those who live solely by Christ's deeds for their sake, the members of the church belong together, as members of the body exist only as parts of the one body and are nothing if severed from that body. Thus participation in Christ's body, i.e., in Christ's sacrifice and victory, which blesses and challenges us, means at the same time participation in the life of all fellow members.

Thus a most interesting development of language leads to new insights. The body of Christ idea underlines the total dependence of the church on Christ's deeds for its sake. But the word "body" means in the Greek language of that time "unity," as it is illustrated by the image of the human body in which all members co-operate. Therefore both statements are made in the same expression: the church lives exclusively by Christ's sacrifice and resurrection; and it does so exclusively in the mutual love of its many members helping one another and being helped by one another.

We now understand why Paul fought so vehemently against a Lord's Supper which would be understood as a mere sacrament, in which the participants would neglect their brotherhood to the extent of not waiting for latecomers with the common meal. A mystical communion might be experienced individually. The sacramental tokens and the individual believer are the only elements absolutely necessary for this experience. Whether or not the initiate recognizes his fellow believers make no difference. This was true for Gnostic communities. But participation in Christ's body means living by his sacrifice for the world. How could we do so, except in our real, concrete life, and this means: how could we do so, without taking seriously our fellowmen? If, in the Lord's Supper, we are constituted as his body, if we are given there our life because he surrendered his life for our sake, we do so at the concrete table on which bread and wine stay. How could we flee into a mere spirituality, forgetting those who most concretely are sitting at this table or are waiting to sit there? Thus the church cannot be one body except by living in Christ, as Christ's body. And it cannot live as Christ's body except by being one body.

IV *The Church as the Body of Christ*

IN 1 CORINTHIANS 12, COLOSSIANS, AND EPHESIANS

First, we shall try to understand some of the theological and practical consequences of the Pauline concept of the body of Christ for the life of the church. Second, we shall investigate the further development of this idea in the Letters to the Colossians and Ephesians.

We have just stated that the body of Christ idea implied two main views of the church: first, the total dependance of the church on Jesus Christ, his death, and his resurrection; second, the church's unity expressing itself in mutual brotherly help and love. Both sides are particularly exposed by Paul in 1 Corinthians 12.

As in other parts of this letter, Paul is disputing a misunderstanding of the church and its life in Corinth. The Corinthians identified the Spirit of God with supernatural phenomena. Therefore they considered speaking in tongues or miraculous healing as the highest gifts of the Spirit.

In opposition to such a view, Paul, in the first three verses of this chapter, reminds the Corinthians that they experienced unusual "supernatural" gifts also in the time of their former heathen life. They were drawn to their gods by a superhuman power of ecstasy and enthusiasm.

57

There is hence only one mark distinguishing God's Spirit from so many other questionable spirits, namely the confession "Jesus is Lord." If the Spirit really leads to confessing Jesus as Lord, by word and deed, then it is God's Spirit. If it does not, if it leads for instance to boasting on one's religious activities and astonishing miracles, it is certainly not God's Spirit. Or to express the same thought in other words: if the result of the Spirit's activity is the building up of the whole church, it is God's Spirit. If not, it is a foreign and evil spirit.

This is the way in which Paul states it in verse 7 and in the 14th chapter. At this point Paul threw the switch to the right track for centuries of theological thinking. The question of whether the Christian life shows more or less enthusiasm, more or less soberness, is at least no primary question, and depends much more on climate, heritage, tradition, and education than on possessing more or less of divine Spirit. People in the southern, Italian-speaking part of even this small country of Switzerland, where at least an owner of an *American* car must be careful not to violate the borderline when backing out of his garage, are living with much more enthusiasm and experiencing everything, including their encounter with God, much more intensely than we in the more northern, German-speaking parts. Such natural predispositions may be used by God as well as by the devil, whether they be of an enthusiastic sort or of a sober and critical mind. If a member of the church is able to pray in moving words which touch the heart, in jubilant praise, even shifting to speaking in tongues, it may be the sign of the presence of God's Spirit, or it may be the sign of an unsteady mind possessed by an unsound desire to impose upon other people. If a member of the church is extremely sober, even critical in his mind, it may be the gift of God's Spirit, edifying the whole congregation, or it may be the expression of a coolness of heart which is much more interested in his own affairs than in God's. Thus the only relevant question is whether or not our enthusiasm or our soberness is used in order to proclaim Jesus as Lord and thereby to build up the church.

This understanding of the Spirit of God enables the apostle to take all spiritual gifts seriously. In 12:4-6 he uses three significative synonyms for these gifts. They are first "gifts of grace," an expression which underlines the fact that they are not man's talents, but God's actions, even if God uses very often man's natural abilities or his education. They are secondly "services," stressing the indispensable openness toward the fellow members. Thirdly, the gifts are called "actions," a term by which Paul shows that any ministry in the church is to be thought of as an event rather than as an official position or dignity with privileges and rights unaltered for a lifetime or even for centuries. At the same time these three verses form a kind of trinitarian statement, mentioning the Spirit as the giver of the "gifts of grace" which are not man's own abilities, the Lord Jesus as the one to whom all "services" are rendered, because he himself gave the first example of service, and God the continual Creator of all life-giving action.

However, Paul is not interested in an ontological doctrine of the Trinity, but rather in the fact that God encounters man time and time again in different ways, as the Spirit, as the Lord Jesus, and as the Creator, being always the one God. Verse 7 sums it up: the manifestation of the same Spirit is given to every single member of the church.

This is an extremely important statement for Paul. So important is it that he repeats it time and again in his letters, and he, consciously or unconsciously, avoids using a special word for "official" ministries, like that of a pastor or a bishop. For a special term like the German "*Amt*," or even the English "ministry" in its usual sense, would easily lead to a concept of the church in which official services like that of a bishop were considered to have a sort of dignity which services such as intercession or special faith (verse 9) would not possess.

There are four different terms in Greek for an official ministry, and at least one of them, common to the Old Testament texts, is very often used in the New Testament (*leitourgia*). The astonishing discovery, however, is the insight that all New Testament writers agree in using this word exclusively for the ministry of the Jewish priests, of the Roman government, or of the church as a whole, but never for the ministry of any individual. The same is true for all derivations of the same root, adjective and verb. The sole exception is Romans 15:16 where Paul uses once the personal noun "minister" for his own apostleship in a very exceptional passage to which I called attention in *New Testament Studies*, 8, pp. 1 ff. To this extent is the New Testament church apprehensive of giving an official character to a particular ministry which would suggest some superiority as compared with other unofficial ministries.

In principle, all ministries in the one body of Christ are on the same level. This is shown by the list of the various gifts in verses 8-11. There is no hierachy of gifts, and the sequence of the mentioned services is given more or less at random. It is quite different in Romans 12:6-8 or even at the end of 1 Corinthians 12. One thing, however, is clear: speaking in tongues ranges at the end of the list, not because Paul despises it—1 Corinthians 14:5 is proof to the contrary—but precisely because the Corinthians overvalued it, in spite of the fact that it is of no help to others.

Out of the same reason, both passages which deal with the ministries in the church lead to the praise of love (Rom. 12:8—13:10; 1 Cor. 13) as the one gift which is also the reason that the gift of the understandable word, particularly the prophecy, ranges usually at the first place (Rom. 12:6; 1 Cor. 12:8, 28; 14:1 ff.). It is the most valuable gift, since more than other gifts it serves all other members of the church.

In opposition to the emphasis on the primacy of speaking in tongues, Paul also includes helpers and administrators in his list. That these ministries, too natural, too worldly, in the sight of the Corinthians, were not pursued in Corinth, is proved by verses 29 and 30. For Paul goes on saying that of course not everybody can be an apostle or a prophet, etc., repeating the whole list of gifts with the sole exception of the helpers and administrators. Obviously nobody wanted to do such a profane service which promised so little religious splendor and glory.

The center of the whole chapter is verses 12 and 13. It is here that the foundation of all the different practical assertions becomes visible. Verse 12 contains the image of the human body which has many members and yet is one. The amazing fact is the end of the verse where Paul does not say, as we should expect: ". . . so it is with the church." He says: ". . . so is Christ" (author's translation). This shows how deeply the apostle's conviction is rooted in the faith that the church is living entirely by Christ's own life in it. Hence the different members of the church with their various contributions to the life of the congregation can be one because they are one in Jesus Christ. He was crucified and raised from the dead long before they were even born. As human beings they may be very different, even incompatible with one another. And yet in baptism they have been incorporated into the body of Christ, into that realm of blessing and challenge which henceforth is the sole basis of their existence. In the life of the church they must therefore make manifest only what is fundamentally true, since the death and resurrection of Jesus Christ created the church.

All that Paul writes about the various gifts, about their fundamental equivalence and their character as services to fellowmen, is only understandable if we realize how self-evident it is for him that all activities of the church are the activities of Christ himself, and that hence neither boasting nor depression is thinkable in the church.

This is described at some length in the following parable of the human body. As it should be in the church, the first address in verses 15-20 is given to the members who cannot cope with their inferiority complexes, while the second part in verses 21-25 fights against the conceited members.

In the church, as in a human body, every member is important. Certainly the ears may be hidden beneath some strange new fashion of hairdressing. Certainly a friend looks into the eyes of his friend and not into his

ears. But this in no way alters the fact that ears are also
of highest importance for the life of the body. For, argues
Paul, what would a body be, if consisting exclusively of
an eye? It would simply be an abortion, a spectacle to be
preserved in alcohol for medical students interested in
utterly abnormal deformities.

In the same way a church consisting only of a highly
revered pastor—or an utmost efficient organizer or a
most important financial genius who knows how to run
a church—and some very unimportant appendages would
actually be but an abortion.

Therefore the Corinthians are fundamentally and primarily the body of Christ, and only in a secondary way
individual members (verse 27). The main reality is the
oneness of Christ's body. The individuality of the members is only a secondary characteristic of the one body.

We shall never understand the nature of the human
body if we begin thinking about the single members
severed from the body and try to conceive of the body as
a mere sum of hundreds of those members. We shall
never understand Paul's concept of the church if we
begin our theological thinking with the individual Christian and consider the church as something like a social
gathering or an association of individuals sharing some
common interests.

And yet, the unity of this church is neither mysterious
nor mystical. It is based on the historical event of a
shameful and painful death and of God's subsequent
deed of resurrection happening in a specific place of our
earth on a specific date of our chronology. It must be
lived time and time again anew in that faith to which
Paul summons his readers.

Years passed on. The problems of the church did not always and everywhere remain the same. In Asia Minor some ten or twenty years afterward, quite different questions arose. It was no more the meaning of Christ for the local congregation that was the central issue, it was more and more the problem of what Jesus Christ meant for the world, for the whole cosmos.

Hellenistic men found this one of their most urgent problems. More and more they realized that man was unable to cope with his world. Supermen like Alexander the Great arose in the political arena. Giant armies of mercenaries conquered the earth. No individual bravery was of any help. The minute states that the Greek cities formed were totally unable to influence the political and military events. The feeling of being helplessly and hopelessly delivered up to a blind destiny grew stronger and stronger.

The same was true for the area of nature. Man realized more and more that he was no longer able to control the powers of nature. There were mysterious hidden powers unable to be understood by laymen, even if the specialists pretended to explain them. The scientists proved that the moon influenced the tides of the sea and the illnesses of men. And the astrologists drew the logical conclusion, willingly accepted by almost everybody, that the eternal, immovable courses of the stars determined the destiny of men. Heaven became more and more a mere sky, brazen, blind to the agonies of men, deaf to their cries, impenetrable for their prayers. What did Jesus Christ mean for such a world?

Let us begin with a hymn which has been inserted by the author to the Colossians into his letter. Whether this author is Paul in his later years or, as I still think, an intimate disciple of his, is of no relevance in our context. Almost all scholars agree that behind the passage, Colossians 1:15-20, there is a considerable amount of tradition foreign to the theology of the author himself.

To be sure, there is unanimity as to the extent of that tradition. There are approximately a dozen different attempts to reconstruct an original hymn or liturgical sequence in the background of this passage. Why therefore not try for a thirteenth time? This is what I did in *Theologische Literaturzeitung* 1961/4, summarized in the first issue of *New Testament Studies*, 8 (1961/62) pp. 6 ff. Be this as it may, one thing is sure: in the background of this passage, there are definite traces of Hellenistic-Jewish speculations. It seems to me clear that this points to a reinterpretation of Pauline ideas in a Christian congregation which was influenced by such a theology.

If we remember how widely spread the idea of the world as a body, permeated and held together by a divine spirit, was in Hellenistic times, we understand that it was almost inevitable that Hellenistic men would interpret Paul's concept of the body of Christ in this way. For a long time the world had been understood as a living and divine body, or even more precisely as the body of God, even as the body whose head God is. God and world were one in this Greek thinking. This view was thought to be confirmed by Paul's preaching about the body of Christ. The only change would be the substitution of Christ for the rather nebulous Greek deity with the revered old name of "Zeus" or the more modern names like "destiny" or "ether." Then Christ would be understood as this power which holds together and vivifies the whole cosmos.

This idea recommended itself even more, since in pre-Christian Hellenistic Judaism the belief in a heavenly being called Wisdom was widely accepted. This being was pre-existent, co-operating in creation, permeating the whole cosmos, descending to earth, redeeming the world, and ascending into heaven again. The terms of this Wisdom myth presented themselves for describing Christ as the heavenly being whose body consisted of the whole world. In this sense the congregation in Colossae praised Christ in their services in approximately the following words (reconstructed from Colossians 1:15-20):

> He is the image of the invisible God, the first-born of all creation;
>> For in him all things were created, in heaven and on earth,
>>> All things were created through him and for him.
>>> And it is he who is before all things,
>>> And it is in him that all things hold together,
>>> And it is he who is the head of the body.
> He is the beginning, the first-born from the dead;
>> For in him all the fullness of God was pleased to dwell,
>>> To reconcile all things through him and to him.

In the first part of this hymn the parallels to the Jewish wisdom literature can be quoted almost word by word. The second part considered originally the resurrection of Jesus Christ as the main saving event which reunited the separated spheres of the cosmos, the divine and the human world, the area of heaven and the area of earth. Probably the resurrection of Christ was understood as a physical ascension which reunited earth and heaven and removed all obstacles on the way to heaven, similar to the way in which the fiends, according to the Hellenistic world view, are standing guard in the intermediate sphere of the air, hindering all earthly beings attempting to secure access to the heavenly reaches. At any rate, Easter was considered as a physical or metaphysical event opening the way to heaven. The importance of Christ for the world was thus seen in two physical facts: (1) the world had been created through Christ and was therefore physically his body, and (2) it was reunited with heaven by his physical ascent.

This reinterpretation is not surprising; it is exactly what we should expect when we know all the Hellenistic ideas about the divine Wisdom figure. The really amazing and stimulating thing, however, is the way in which the author to the Colossians took up and corrected this view. Not being a modern author who has the means of footnotes at his disposition, he inserts first some small comments into the original hymn. They have been left out in the preceding reconstruction of this passage. The fact that the phrases disturbing the perfect parallelism of these verses manifest also a distinctly different theological point of view gives some probability to such a separation of the original hymn from the additions by the author of the letter. The same theology appears secondly in the commentary which he gives at the end of our passage and in some later paragraphs of his letter. Even scholars who are more skeptical than I regarding a reconstruction of an original hymn would agree that there

is a mixture of a strictly Hellenistic-Jewish background
with some definitely Pauline ideas.

The author to the Colossians certainly does not totally
oppose such a reinterpretation of the body of Christ concept, as it had been shaped in Colossae. Indeed, Christ
is of importance not only for the church, but also for the
whole cosmos. Indeed, he is permeating the world. Indeed, he is the sole salvation for all creatures. Indeed, he
is Lord over all powers, over nature as well as over
supermen and demons. And yet, this praise of his
sovereignty is in some way also wrong. On three main
points, the author of the letter corrects this rather over-
enthusiastic Colossian hymn.

First, this hymn proclaims that all things have been
reconciled with God in Christ. This is an assertion which
is unique in the New Testament. For the Colossians, it
was the logical consequence of their understanding of
the saving event of the resurrection. If by it earth and
heaven have been physically or metaphysically reunited,
then of course every single thing on earth has been reconciled with God.

The author of our letter, however, distinguishes clearly
between Christ the head of his body the church and
Christ the head over all powers. Originally the Colossian
hymn hailed Christ as the head of the world-body. Our
author gives his own interpretation of the body of Christ
as the church, adding to verse 18a the words "namely
the church." He says exactly the same in 1:24, and he
makes his meaning quite clear in 2:10: Christ is the head
over all rule and authority because, as 2:15 explains, he
disarmed the principalities and powers in his ascension
after his death on the cross. So far this agrees with the
Colossians.

Whereas Paul, in his undisputed letters, is more cautious and speaks of the final subjection of all powers only in the context of the parousia (1 Cor. 15:25 ff.), he draws the conclusion from texts like Romans 8:38: Since this final victory of Christ is absolutely sure, one may also say that the powers have already been made subject by him. For Christ is certainly even Lord over all the world, as he is over the church.

And yet, there is a difference between those who acknowledge his lordship and are connected with him like a body with its head, and those who do not. He is Lord also for the latter and they will realize that in the end, but at present they are not yet so closely associated with him as is his body, the church. Colossians 2:15 most certainly does not describe a reconciliation, but a subjection of all the powers and authorities. The author stresses his understanding by inserting the phrase "that in all things he might have the pre-eminence" (1:18, K.J.V.) and particularly by his commentary in 1:21 where he does not speak of "all things," but of the converted Gentiles who have been reconciled by Christ.

Second, the Colossian hymn focused on the resurrection. This only could be understood as a physical miracle that changed the state of the world and its relation to heaven. The commentator, however, inserts the reference to the cross into the very hymn itself, and he expands this in his following explications in 1:22. By doing this he changes the whole meaning. Gnosticism failed to cope with the cross, as the texts of the second and the third centuries show. The same would be true for Christianity as the Colossians understood it, a Christianity which pretended to give the absolute guaranty for salvation as soon as one took the miracle of the resurrection uniting heaven and earth for granted and was sacramentally united with the Head residing already in the divine sphere above.

A theology in the center of which the cross stands is clearly distinguished from such a view. Certainly the death of Jesus on the cross is an objective fact in history, no less objective than the resurrection. Certainly what God did in this death is irreversibly valid, valid for the whole world. And yet its effect is not the effect of a mere physical event, independent of whether one hears about it and understands it or not. It does not work like, to use a Gnostic image, a magnet put up in heaven and drawing those who are brought into its magnetic field irresistibly after it. The effect of Christ's death is the effect of a deed of love bringing its fruit in a human life which is touched by it.

If a mother works hard for the loaf of bread that she brings in the evening to her children, this bread nourishes all her children equally; still, it makes an enormous difference whether or not a child perceives the whole love of the mother in her offering of the slice of bread. Only the child who realizes the amount of love in the background of the evening meal is actually brought into such a fellowship with the mother that it would be comparable to the unity of Head and body in the sense of the letter written to the Colossians. To be sure, even this understanding is not the child's own work, but the result of the love of the mother given to him.

Thus, reconciliation is certainly totally God's work done in Jesus Christ, but it reaches into our very life, into the center of our personality where it creates its own echo. Hence reconcilation must, according to Colossians, not be thought of in terms of physical or metaphysical events which would automatically change everything and guarantee salvation if only one will take these facts for granted and make sure to participate in their result by means of sacramental union. Rather it must be conceived in terms of human relationships, of deeds of love done by one to another. If a wife does a deed of love for her husband, this is certainly an objective fact which changes something. And yet, all the world depends on whether or not her husband sees her love in this deed. It could lead him into inferiority complexes or into an attitude of resentment and shame. And it could lead him into an understanding of love which frees him and makes him happy. Therefore her deed of love is not finished with the objective deed. She will accompany her husband and help him to interpret her deed as a liberating deed of love and not as a humiliating act of charity.

Hence, faith is not simply belief that such and such events really took place, or that such and such interpretation is the orthodox one, or that such and such sacraments are effective. Faith includes the wholeness of a life which is changed by the love expressed in these events, in Jesus Christ, and accompanying the believer day by day, in the Holy Spirit. It is belief in Jesus Christ and in the Holy Spirit. This love of God is the only real guaranty, not any fact or event which is merely to be taken for granted or appropriated by means of sacraments.

As long as we do not see this love of God in events and facts and are not touched by it, it does not help to believe in them, to understand them correctly, and to use the sacraments regularly. Hence a proclamation of the resurrection without a proclamation of the cross of Jesus would be equally as wrong as contrariwise. Therefore the commentary in 1:22, 23, speaks of Christ's death on the cross and of faith and obedience on the part of the church. Also in 2:14 the cross of Jesus is introduced as the basis of verse 15 which originally spoke of Christ's ascent only.

Third, the writer of this letter clarifies his understanding of the topic of Christ permeating the world. Indeed, Christ permeates the world, not merely the church. But he does so not as a mysterious spiritual power, found everywhere as was the divine spirit of the Stoic philosophers which permeated stones, plants, animals, and men. Christ permeates the world, as the commentary in 1:23 explains, in the apostle's mission to which the congregation contributes by its prayers and its gifts, and by the actual accompanying of the apostle by the members. The cosmic dimension of this mission is also stressed in 1:6. In 1:25-27 a new theological idea is connected with it. These verses understand the Christ event as the divine revelation of the mystery of God hidden for ages, revealed in Christ, and conquering the whole world in the mission. Such an understanding is rooted in Jewish apocalypticism expecting the disclosure of all mysteries in the end, and in Jewish wisdom literature considering the Wisdom as the divine revealer of the life-giving wisdom of God. In Colossians 2:2 ff. it is expressed in the very words of this sapiental literature.

This is a most important theological development. Henceforth the topic of the revealed mystery and of the mission to the whole world appears time and again not only in admonitions to the church, but even in the very creeds themselves. This is obvious in Ephesians, especially in 2:11—3:13, where the conversion of the Gentiles is the very content of the theological thinking. The same terminology, the mystery kept secret to the sons of man in other generations, but revealed to the apostle, appears and is referred to in the context of the mission to the Gentiles and even to the principalities and powers (3:3-6, 8-16). Here again it seems that this mission was originally connected in a primitive way with the triumphal ascent of Christ. The unexpected formulation of 2:17 and the parallels in Schlier's commentary make this at least probable.

Much more important is 1 Timothy 3:16. It is a hymn, quoted verbatim, and considered as the "mystery" accepted unanimously by the whole church as its creed. This again is a highly Hellenized form of the Christian belief. It speaks shortly in the first line of Christ's epiphany in the flesh, and in the other five lines of his triumphal ascension. Again some mythological ideas seem to lie in the background. The "angels" to whom Christ appeared in his ascension are probably the powers that he conquered when passing through the spheres between earth and heaven. The decisive fact, however, is the way in which this hymn interprets this triumphant procession of Christ. It takes place, first of all, in the context of the mission to all nations. Both Christ's ascension to heaven and his victorious march to the farthest ends of the earth are seen together and interwoven in a way which no more cares for any chronological sequence: He appeared to the angels—was proclaimed to the nations—was believed on in the world—was taken up into the glory.

An analysis of the redactional passages in Mark's Gospel, which I tried to present in *Evangelische Theologie*, June 1964, shows how central the concept of the divine mystery hidden to all mankind, but revealed in the mighty teaching of Jesus and proclaimed in the kerygma of the universal church to all nations, has become for Mark. Finally the same topic appears in the doxology of Romans 16:25-27, which has been added later to the Pauline letter. Again it speaks of the Christ event as of "the mystery . . . kept secret for long ages, but . . . now disclosed," and again, according to this passage, the mystery "is made known to all nations."

SUMMARY

This is the final step in a long and rich development. It started with the Old Testament background of the first Christians, when man was understood primarily in his relation to God and his fellowmen, not as a "body" that would be a world of its own, more or less perfect in and of itself. The first step was the fact that the church learned from its master to see the body as the means of rendering service to others. Even before the time of the New Testament one spoke occasionally about giving up one's body for the sake of others, although very rarely.

When the term "body" appeared Sunday by Sunday during the Lord's Supper in the recitation of the words of institution, it was shaped more and more by this usage. Thus, the understanding of the body as the means of communication, even of service to others, became predominant in the New Testament church, since it confessed that its life was completely dependent on Christ's giving up his body for its sake.

The second step was the discussion of Paul with the Corinthians. Meeting for the first time an utterly Hellenized overvaluation of the soul, combined with a contempt of the body, Paul had to stress the understanding of man's body as the place in which he encounters God and his neighbors. Paul, with his Old Testament background, did not see the body as a mere part of man, but as one aspect of his whole personality which was so very important, since faith necessarily requires bodily manifestations as soon as it is lived in the togetherness with other men, whether in church or world.

Hence, "body" is understood by Paul as man in his relation to God and his fellowmen; man as belonging either to God or to sin, either to his neighbor or to an egotism in which he sees nothing beyond himself; man as experiencing either God or the devil; man as obeying either his Lord or evil powers; man as loving either others or himself. Hence man is seen primarily not as an individual, but as a being in communication with God and other men. This is the first and theologically important result of our investigation of the New Testament understanding of the body.

The next step of this development leads to the understanding of the church as the body of Christ. There were, as we have seen, at least three different roots which helped to create this expression: (1) the fact that in the church Jesus' crucified body was still present in its blessing and challenge, (2) the pattern of the patriarch containing his whole people in himself, and (3) the Greek phrase "one body" designating a unity consisting of various members.

Hence the second result of theological relevance is a new understanding of the church. Both sides are stressed in the newly coined expression "body of Christ": (1) The church is totally dependent on the crucified and risen body of Christ, i.e., on the saving events which took place at a specific time in a specific place within our history. This dependence on God's act is underlined by the fact that it is primarily in the Eucharist that this character of the "body of Christ" is given to the church. (2) And yet, being the body of Christ is not a mysterious

experience, but is lived day by day in the "bodily" manifestations of the church's faith, namely in the concrete
brotherhood in which obedience to the Lord is manifest
in love to the brothers.

The understanding of this latter idea is reached in two
different steps. Since the term "body of Christ" describes
Christ in his for-our-sake-ness, it would be logical to
understand the church as the body of Christ in such a
way that it would be seen primarily in its openness for
others, for the world, therefore, in its mission to the
nations and its self-sacrifice to those who are outside of
it.

This understanding is actually reached in the Letters
to the Colossians and Ephesians. The first stage of the
development, however, was determined by the wide-
spread Greek image of the body as an organism in which
all the different members are working together in dependence on one another. Therefore, in the usage of the
body of Christ phrase, the interest first in the indisputed
letters of Paul focused on the local congregation in which
every single member lives to the benefit of all fellow
members. The necessity that the whole of this body also
render service to the world was by no means forgotten.
Paul often mentions this, and, to be sure, within passages
dealing with the body of Christ. However, the mission-
ary imperative or the praise of Christ's victory in the
mission to the nations was not yet central in these
passages, because it had not yet been connected with the
very image of the body of Christ.

Therefore, it is only the Letters to the Colossians and
Ephesians which form the last link in the chain. Contrary
to the general view, this is true, not because the concept

of the body of Christ reaches here the depth of a mystery no longer expressed in logical terms, but only to be experienced in a sacramental union. It is true because exactly in these letters, the church is understood as the body of Christ because of its obedience to its Head. The church manifests itself in the mission to the nations, i.e., in its openness and service to the world.

Passages like Colossians 1:24, inserted between verses 23 and 25-27 dealing with Paul's mission to the Gentiles, warn against a misunderstanding of this mission in which the church would feel superior and rich, and underline the unity of mission to the world and self-sacrificing in suffering. This means that the last result of this investigation is the insight that the church can be the body of Christ only if it is willing to suffer and thereby to be the body of its Lord who, in his body, goes into the world, serving all mankind. If the church is willing to live in this way as Christ's body, often suffering and dying, it will experience time and again that he himself creates in it that obedience and that readiness for self-sacrifice, in which he as its Lord encounters the world and converts Gentiles into members of his body.

In this manner the whole history of Greek thinking about the body, from Homer up to the late Stoic philosophers in the time of the New Testament, provided the philosophical tools for understanding and the linguistic means for expressing the old Hebrew thought that man must be considered primarily not as an individual being complete in itself, but in *his responsibility to God and his relation to his fellowmen.*

260
Sch4

Date Due